Eye Contact Training

Learn How To Attract Women

+

Improve Your Self Confidence, Charisma & Leadership

Robert Moore

Robert Moore

Table of Contents

Robert Moore

Introduction

Hey badass!

First, I want to thank you and congratulate you for purchasing "Eye Contact Training".

As you probably know, the eyes are the windows to the soul. Every person, male or female, can literally feel your soul just looking at your eyes.

Now, I could end the whole book right here.

Since YOU deserve more value, however, I'm going to give you a fu*kton of it.

Are you ready? This stuff will change your business life, your social life and your interactions with the other gender.

If you always found yourself turning your head because you felt embarrassed to look directly in the eyes of a beautiful, attractive girl...

If your eyes usually feel a strong urge to subject in front of your boss, leaving you in a weak, flickering, low status physical and mental position...

Then this book will really transform your life, just like mine got transformed.

First, I'll show you how important inner strength and congruence are for the confident alpha male you'll become.

Then, I will teach you how to handle the tension in high-pressure situations, making yourself stand out as a real badass every time you have the opportunity.

I will give you simple yet effective exercises, in order to master the skill of always holding a strong, deep and powerful eye contact, no matter who you're talking to.

Everyone can do them, so do not hold back and start DOMINATING your life!

Thanks again, I hope you enjoy this guide!

The Power To Attract

"Attraction isn't a choice." – David DeAngelo

David DeAngelo nailed it on the head when he wrote a book with the same title. Attraction isn't something that's deliberate...at least for the person who is attracted. No woman ever said "Hey! I will turn on my attraction buttons for that rich, fat slob over there!" It just doesn't work that way.

Case in point – women who swear they want to marry the "good guys". When I say good guys, I didn't mean cops, bro! I didn't mean men who are dressed like Superman either – they with pants first, underwear second.

You know what I'm talking about. Guys who are bashful, courteous, cultured, generous, always available to serve, respectful, prim and proper, has a Master's Degree from Harvard, doesn't smoke, doesn't cuss and certainly doesn't tell green jokes. In other words, the kind of guys women can safely bring home and present to their mommas and poppas.

Unfortunately, it's usually the parents who like such guys and not the woman herself. Well, they may like such men but they chances are, they aren't attracted.

Whoa, do you mean to say that my having a Master's Degree from Cambridge, my being polite and courteous, my not smoking and my not drinking alcohol, among other things, won't make that woman that I'm attracted to be attracted to me? How can that be? That's preposterous! If you ask women what the qualities they want in their future husbands, those qualities are right at the top! Don't all women want to marry the good guys – the nice guys?

Yes, that's what I mean.

Case in point: rock stars. They're quite an arrogant, narcissistic, rude and pompous bunch, are they not? But honestly, who gets to bang the most women, who by the way aren't bad looking at all? Who are the men many supermodels fall for and couldn't seem to let go of?

Rock stars.

Ok, you can make the case that these guys are famous and loaded. You have a point there. Nothing that millions of dollars can't fix or compensate for, right? Probably.

But consider some of my closest women friends who are beautiful and not to mention smart. They're smart in all areas except when it comes to men. I'll share with you the story of two of my closest female friends who are both smart, achievers and beautiful who both fell hard – and continue to struggle with letting go – for men who are anything but ideal.

My first friend, let's hide her under the name Dianne. She's a serious Christian who has turned her back on the ways of the world for many, many years now. She's now at the point wherein she wants to marry. And considering where she is in her faith now, she has very high standards.

Oh, and she has a very strong personality. So strong that as beautiful and well known as she is in church, very few men, if any, had the guts to even ask her out.

Enter George, a former leader in her church who has fallen from grace. He used to be a campus missionary who slid back into "worldly" living and by that I mean sex, bikes and rock and roll. He's trying to get back into the good graces of Dianne's church and was welcomed back. He met Dianne at a post-church service get together.

He couldn't take his eyes off her. Unfortunately, part of his falling from grace is his looks. He looks nowhere near the former hunk he used to be. He gained some weight and now keeps a relatively unkempt look. He isn't ugly but he's no longer that "hunky". So when he asked Dianne to go out, Dianne politely declined. Then George asked her out again and even asked within a few days of meeting her if he can court her. Again, the answers were no. But he remained unperturbed.

And they went out. Within a week or two, she had fallen for him. The serious Christian woman who's ready to get married and is waiting for that "godly" man to come fell for a backslidden man who's just a shadow of his former religious and hunky self. What just happened there?

My other friend, let's call her Melanie. Melanie's also quite a beautiful woman who has a master's degree from a reputable university in Seattle. She's the only child of very rich parents, with her dad being a senior partner in one of the country's biggest law firms. Oh, she's also a deeply religious woman.

Enter Jordan, one of her officemates. Jordan is quite the success story. Coming from a financially challenged and dysfunctional family, he did well in school and landed a prestigious position in the same government office that Melanie works in. He's very good at what he does and as such, he was given a 1-year Master's Degree scholarship in London courtesy of that government office.

The thing with Jordan is he may be an achiever, quite financially desirable but he's one very big walking ego. If there was a Guinness World Record for biggest ego, I'm pretty sure he'd be one of the top contenders for it. He would run to Melanie when he's down, which is supposedly often, and tell her how much he misses her but at the same time would divulge to her all his sexual trysts with other women. What a pig! But a chick-magnet pig!

As with Dianne, Melanie fell for the S.O.B. and she fell hard. In fact, she fell in too deep that after almost a year after I confronted the guy to leave her be, she's still in love with him.

If nice guys don't finish last – at least in the attraction business – then why is it George and Jordan are able to attract women, even those who are looking to marry "nice guys"?

That's what David DeAngelo meant by attraction isn't a choice. Once you push her buttons, it doesn't matter if you're an angel or the incarnation of the devil himself. You got her hooked!

Robert Moore

Push The Button

"If you're ready for me boy, you'd better push the button and let me know." – Sugababes, Push The Button

When I ride the lift in my apartment building, it moves a certain way. If I push the "up" button while waiting at the ground floor, it's a matter of time before the lift – or elevator as the Americans call it more often – stops at the ground floor, opens its doors to welcome me in. Once inside, I push another button – this time the floor where I want to get off. Again, the lift has no choice but respond accordingly and go to the floor I specified. It opens and I get off. Unless another person in another floor pushes a button, the elevator stays still.

It's like that with people.

When certain people are able to push our attraction buttons, our responses are most often automatic. Well, at least internally. Have you ever experienced being madly in love with someone? If you have, then you would probably agree with me when I say that such attraction wasn't something you asked for. I mean c'mon, do you actually pray to God to make you so attracted to that girl in your class who has a super pretty face, hot body and the sex appeal of a Playboy bunny? I didn't think so. Have you ever been in a committed relationship but still you find yourself irresistibly attracted to another woman, much to your chagrin and resistance? You can control your reaction but you weren't able to control how you felt, right? It's because they pushed the right buttons and elicited that internal reaction.

Don't think that it's just us dudes who are "automatic". Women are too! However, men and women have a different set of buttons and that's what we'll discuss in this chapter together with how to push their buttons for our advantage.

MALE BUTTON: LOOKS

For us guys, the main attraction buttons are, surprise, looks. In fact, how easy it is for us to get an erection and feel an irresistible urge to either bang away or romanticize our hand when in the midst of a really hot woman. No, it doesn't matter if she mixes up her "f" and "p" (don't forget to fay the bills, dear!) or prefers to have a whole pizza sliced into 4 slices instead of 8 because she can only finish four slices. If she looks hot enough, we're hooked!

Without meaning to demean our species, that's how we men are attracted – visually. To paraphrase Lady Gaga's hit song, we were born this way. How I wish we could say "Her emotional quotient or her doting motherly nature just turns me on!" Nope, that's not how we roll, guys.

FEMALE BUTTON: PERSONALITY

Many times, I'd run into couples in a mall or in bars where a hot woman is all over her not so hot (at least physically) man. I go like "What manner of narcotics is this woman on, dawg?" It don't make common sense, ya' dig?

Then I look back on the two lady friends I mentioned earlier – Dianne and Melanie. Dianne tried to push George back, not being her physical, spiritual and financial type at all! Melanie, though a bit more passive, was totally pissed at Jordan for having the gall to tell her he misses her one second only to tell her of his sexual contests and projects the next. These guys are supposed to be – at least based on what our moms tell us – at the bottom of the romantic food chain, right? But no, they're on top! Then it hit me about what David DeAngelo wrote on attraction from a women's perspective: it's all about personality. And in particular, it's about confidence.

THE GREAT DIVIDE

Robert Moore

Allow me to wax geeky for a moment here but I'd like to talk about one of the most basic and profound economic principles: supply and demand.

Simply stated, the scarcer a thing is relative to demand, the higher its perceived value becomes. The more abundant it becomes relative to demand, the lower its perceived value becomes. This principle explains why charcoal and diamonds, though both are primarily made from carbon, are galaxies apart in terms of price. Coal is just too abundant in supply while diamonds are too scarce.

Now why on earth did I have to bring up that principle? Well, this is for you to better understand the principles that govern attraction, particularly for women. Think of you and other men as either coals or diamonds. What determines your value or attractiveness to women is your scarcity – your uniqueness. By being scarce, I mean you're different from all the other men that she normally comes into social or physical contact with. And it's that difference that can turn her attraction buttons on. Take note, I said "can" and not "will". Why?

Well, it depends on how different you are from the rest of the average male species. You can be different in an attractive way and you can be attractive in a creepy, repulsive way.

So what separates the sheep from the goat, the puppies from the wolves and unattractive men from attractive ones? From a woman's perspective – confidence.

Yes, confidence.

According to David DeAngelo, the key things women are looking for in a guy's personality are:

-They're in control of the situation;

-They're in control of themselves (men); and

-They're in control of them (women).

Men and women are wired differently with men being the protector and provider while women are the nurturer or care giver. As generations passed, however, society has evolved to the point that most men have been emasculated or robbed of their manly strength and power. I think in particular, this is the effect of video games and porn addiction! And as more and more women started to enjoy flourishing careers and sexual equality, more men became emasculated. As more men became emasculated, women continued to have a harder time finding a man who'll make them feel secure and protected and so they learned to fend for themselves. In this day and age, however, being able to do that comes with a lot of pleasurable rewards and as such, women have become more and more independent to the point that they feel they hardly need men.

To aggravate this situation, we've been taught that to make the women of our dreams be attracted to us, we must please them in every possible way. Be nice, be polite, be courteous, be generous, be pleasant, be unobtrusive and always give her what she needs and wants. As more and more men succumbed to this "wisdom", society has grown armies of emasculated men even more!

So can you imagine, women becoming more independent and men becoming more sissies? You have a shortage of manly men that women are attracted to! Remember the economic principle of supply and demand? Ah yes...now you see why I had to incorporate such a scholastic principle to our carnal discussion, eh?

To make this discussion a bit closer to home, let's hark back to my two close female friends. Remember Dianne and how many guys are attracted to her but are intimidated? Given her strong personality, most men fold when they're with her – she always has her way. Because most of the men that are attracted to her belong to the sissy army, hardly anyone who wants to win her over ever do so because they're all the same – sissies. Dianne has an over-supply of men she has so much control over, men who show that they're not in control of the situation, themselves and Dianne.

But George was different. True, he wasn't exceptionally good looking. In fact, didn't I say he's just a shadow of his former hunky Godly self? But one thing that separated him from the rest of the Dianne-worshippers pack was his persistence. Remember I said Dianne turned his invitations down several times before saying yes just to shut him up? Dianne didn't intimidate George, and her unconscious mind picked up on that – that he was in control of the situation, of himself and even Dianne.

In short, Dianne's unconscious mind singled out George as different from the rest of her admirers as being the only confident one. By his persistence, he sent the subtle message to Dianne's unconscious mind that he's different, that he's scarce.

He's a diamond among the coals.

The same goes for Melanie and Jordan. Most of the guys that courted Melanie – including her last boyfriend – were polite, courteous and wholesome! Perfect for her mom and dad! And because Melanie grew up in a very strictly controlled household and being an only child at that, she wasn't used to being free and independent. She always had to measure up to people, particularly her parents.

So imagine how different Jordan was from all those men who came before? Sure, he was rude, cocky and a bit assuming but hey, he didn't give a fuck!

And such freedom and lack of concern about what others may say silently screamed about just how confident Jordan is as a man. That he's in control of his situation, himself and even Melanie! Even if Melanie already asked for space, Jordan never respected that. He was the boss. And Melanie was drawn to such confidence and autonomy having never experienced that in her life. Jordan was way different from the crowd. And that pushed her buttons, just like how George pushed Dianne's.

It Starts From Within

"The eyes are the windows of the soul." – Cicero

If this is true, then the primary way eye contact is effective in attracting women and leading people is if the soul that it shows people from within is a confident one.

Make no mistake about it, it's high-status confidence that primarily attracts a woman. You may look as hot as Bradley Cooper but if you don't have confidence and you're a sissy, women won't be attracted to you or will immediately be un-attracted to you.

A neat little prank – with a poignant lesson – that I play on some of the attendees of the talks that I give is that I ask them to hold a piece of candy in front of them, with arms straight and at eye level as I continue giving the talk. They said lifting the candy that way isn't anywhere near difficult, with its very lightweight. But after 5 minutes, their arms aren't as high or as level with their eyes any more and in less than 10 minutes, most of them give up and surrender the candy.

Afterwards, I ask the brave volunteers why they couldn't keep the candy up for long, considering it was a very light object. The discussion would eventually lead to – please bear with me for another geeky principle – gravity.

Gravity is that continuous force that pulls pretty much everything down. It's the reason why things fall down to the earth. It's a relentless force that never rests and never takes a break. That's why it's pretty much impossible to hold a candy that way for long periods of time. It's natural to go down.

Similarly, you can do all the eye contact training that you possibly can but if at the core you have low self-esteem, believe me when I say it's gonna show and women will pick up on that.

Maybe you can fake it till you make it, maybe you can't.

But the bottom line is that your body language and eyes can only consistently reveal what is within. There's no going around it.

So how do you actually build up confidence from within? It begins with knowing about the factors that affect your self-confidence first.

Factors That Affect Your Self Confidence

Many factors influence your self-confidence, some of them you may not be aware of. How much of those factors you're aware of and understand will determine your ability to become as confident as James Bond. Your inability to understand or know some of these factors may mean the difference between being able to successfully make eye contact or not.

FAMILY

One of the major factors that have shaped, or may even continue to shape your self-confidence is your relationship with your family. Your folks, your siblings and even your grandparents have a significant contribution to your level of self-confidence as you know it.

Our most vulnerable moments – personality and psyche wise – is when we're children. It's when our minds are most pliable. Much of what becomes our adult emotional styles, personalities and characters are molded during those times. One way is through imitation. As children, we don't have any idea of what works or what doesn't in the world and so we assume that adults, particularly our parents, have it all figured out and we unconsciously imitate their attitudes, behaviors and even speech. If our parents are shy, bashful and un-assertive, we may grow up thinking that it is the way to live life and that being confident and assertive is from the devil.

Another way is through mental programming, intentional or otherwise. Most parents have the best intentions for their kids, I presume but the greatest of intentions is no match for the smallest of deeds. Many times, our parents raise us up in ways that they deemed best for us (intentions) but there are moments too that because of ignorance, they actually raise us (deed) to not be confident. Unknowingly, they program much of our attitudes, values and personalities directly or indirectly.

My favorite example of this is my own mother. Ever the pessimistic one, she has the best of intentions even when her default mode is to tell me that I will most probably screw things up. She would always say things to me like:

-Better be careful or you'll end up forgetting your umbrella again as you always do.

-What? You, an entrepreneur? You don't have the experience or training for that!

-Let me do it, you don't know how to do it.

All this time, I never thought it had anything to do with how I previously felt about myself – low self-confidence. I used to dread learning new things, reciting in front of the class and volunteering to do a public presentation, among other things. It wasn't until I became conscious about what my unconscious mind actually believed about me that I overcame my lack of self-confidence, though it took some time.

I was also influenced by my parents' lack of social skills, i.e., they were shy. Because I'd see how they react to or avoid being invited to many social gatherings where they didn't know a lot of people, I unconsciously thought that was the norm. Part of my lack of self-confidence before was – guess what? – going to social gatherings where I hardly know anyone.

More is caught than taught.

CLASSMATES AND TEACHERS

Depending on the depth of your relationship with your parents, classmates and teachers can be the next biggest, if not the biggest influence on your self-confidence while growing up.

Many shy, socially awkward people happened to have been bullied or ridiculed for the most part of their school lives. Those experiences helped shaped their view about themselves because for children, the approval of peers is a big deal. That's why there are children who grow up to be socially awkward despite growing up in a caring and encouraging home because let's face it, most of a child's time is spent in school and school is as real as they come. In school, they don't have the benefit of parental support and protection – they're on their own.

When I was but a chubby little kid, I was actually more than chubby – I was obese! Even if my folks didn't nag me about my weight, my classmates often would. I remember that day when one of my guy classmates asked me to jump. When I asked him why should I, he just said jump and he'll tell me. So I jumped...and he and the rest of the gang yelled "man boobs!" That was one of the most humiliating moments of my life that stuck to me even as a young adult. That was one defining moment for my self-confidence, or what was left of it back then.

On the other hand, many of my friends who were the cool and popular people back in school grew up to be either well-adjusted or got into trouble due to overconfidence. My point is, those who were socially validated at school for the most part didn't grow up to be adults with low self-esteem issues, even if they didn't amount to much as adults. The solid foundations of their confidence, as reinforced during their school days, remained despite the changing situations.

MEDIA

You may not be aware but media is a very powerful social conditioning tool. Some even go as far as saying it's mass-brainwashing. I believe it is so. If it isn't, then why would companies all over the world collectively spend billions of dollars annually for advertising?

In Martin Lindstrom's best selling book on consumer behavior "Buy-Ology: Truth And Lies About Why We Buy", he presents scientific evidence about how advertisements – strategically made and placed – do have the subtle and inconspicuous ability to make us buy the products advertised. And part of the feelings that advertisers want to invoke that will eventually lead to our patronizing the products they advertise is being inadequate.

Take for example feminine wash. So what if a woman's peepee doesn't smell naturally nice? What do you expect after wearing underwear all the time, and peeing and when they have their period? But feminine wash advertisers are very effective in making women feel inadequate by making beautiful, sexy women play the role of a woman who looks to be complete and content because of using feminine wash. They would demonize the use of soap to make women feel they're not complete as a person and that they need to use feminine wash to have the perfect peepee. What the? Women were sexy, attractive and had healthy vaginas even before feminine wash came along.

Okay, that wasn't a manly example. Let's try something manly then. Let's talk about...ah...abs! Commercials these days try to manipulate us men into buying junk supplements, worthless exercise machines and even certain cosmetics like facial wash (what do abs have to do with the face?). It's like you don't have abs? You ain't cool – unless you buy these products so you'll be! Heck, people like James Dean and Robert Redford were some of the hottest and sexiest men of their time and they didn't have abs nor the benefit of using facial wash other than soap.

It's not just commercials that are emasculating more men than ever. You have TV shows and movies too! More and more TV shows portray men as the "wives" in a marriage instead of the leader that they should be. I'm not trying to be chauvinistic here but that's the natural order of a family, the guy leads. And I'm willing to go out on a limb here that deep inside, many wives and girlfriends or women fuck buddies wish their men are the leaders in their relationships.

Do you see where I'm driving at? If you're not aware, these TV shows, movies, commercials and advertisements will continue pounding away at your self-confidence. Knowledge is power indeed!

PERSONAL EXPERIENCES

What happened to you and the rewards or consequences of your decisions or actions also have a great impact on your self-confidence. In fact, it may even be more powerful than the encouraging or discouraging things that people may say about or do to you. There's a saying that to see is to believe and experiences are powerful "seeings".

I don't want to sound like a religious bigot here but a great example of this would be one's belief or non-belief in the idea of a god. Many strongly believe in one because they experienced what can only be described as "miracles" in their lives – things they couldn't attribute to natural order. Many atheists, as the protagonist Professor Radison portrayed by Kevin Sorbo said in the 2014 movie God's Not Dead said, used to believe in God until God disappointed them. In the case of Professor Radison, he prayed to God to save his dying mom. His mom died, which made him believe that his belief in God is not grounded on truth, hence is passionate advocacy of dissuading those who continue to believe in God from continuing so.

If to see is to believe, then experience always trumps words. And this is the reason why people grew up to be the way they are – personal experiences. I'm not saying you have no power to override your experiences' effects on you. I'm just saying that it does have a great effect on your self-confidence.

Translated into being an alpha male, you may find it quite hard to win chicks over or lead a team because you remember your experiences when women always turned you down or dropped you like a hot potato as what you called a relationship progressed. Particularly if you were dropped very hard, it can be quite a traumatic experience.

The good news is actual experiences aren't the final authority on your self-confidence. It's because, as I'll explain later, experiences can also be manufactured to your advantage.

Developing Your Inner Game

"If you have inner peace, nobody can force you to be a slave to outer reality." – Sri Chinmoy

Now that we've established the importance of developing your self-confidence and the factors that have shaped it before even employing eye contact techniques for seduction and leadership, you'll learn how to develop enough self-confidence to successfully execute the eye contact techniques I'll show you later on. Your successful use of the eye contact tips and tricks will further increase your self-confidence and become an upward spiral of manliness that you've never experienced before.

There are two ways to develop your self-confidence: mental and physical. It's no secret that your physical appearance and movements can affect your confidence and vice versa. So which is which?

It doesn't matter if you start with your mind first or with physical things. What you should remember is that at some point, both will feed off each other. You won't be able to sustain your confidence for long if you don't look and act the part and you won't be able to sustain your confident manly actions and looks if you're not confident inside. Get it?

Here's a simple analogy, although another geeky one. Think of a gas burner. To be able to cook food, you need fire right? Right! In order to set the gas being emitted by your burner on fire, you need fire, which you can create from a match or a lighter. The gas needs fire to create a fire and the created fire needs enough gas to last long. Each feeds of the other. So it is like with your self-confidence and actions.

MINDING YOUR CONFIDENCE

Most psychologists and motivational speakers preach that the mind is functionally divided into, among others, the conscious and the unconscious. The conscious mind is what gives you the ability to reason out and apply logic as you live your life every day. It's also your mental contact point or bridge between the outside world and your unconscious mind, acting as the gatekeeper through which thoughts, words, sensations and experiences are filtered prior to passing through to the unconscious. It's also what helps you control your movements (flexing and relaxing of muscles), speech and thoughts.

On the other hand as the name suggests, the unconscious mind is that part of your mind that operates incognito or without you having to be aware. It's that part of your mind that's on autopilot, meaning you hardly give any thought or attention to. These include your heart beat, breathing and other skills that require a million other ways to execute and coordinate such as playing basketball ala-Stephen Curry or hitting tennis aces all over the court ala-Serena Williams. The really cool thing about your unconscious mind is that it's responsible for behaviors, bodily processes and chemical reactions that are too many to count!

Your self-confidence and your consistent behavioral habits are primarily controlled by your unconscious mind. Dr. Maxwell Maltz wrote in his book groundbreaking classic boo Psychocybernetics that the reason why people fail to implement lasting life changes in habits and behaviors by trying harder and harder. Interestingly, he also wrote why it seems that breakthroughs come at the most ungodly and unexpected times, particularly when we're not thinking of it.

To cut through all the technical mumbo-jumbo, he likened the conscious and the unconscious mind to Navy personnel who inputs a target's coordinates into a torpedo and the torpedo itself, respectively. The torpedo, once launched, can't be stopped until it acquires the target that is programmed into it. So it is with the unconscious mind. Once it is programmed with the help of our sailor conscious mind, it can't be controlled and will automatically make ways for it to achieve its intended target.

If you, with the help of your conscious mind, program it for confidence, then it's just a matter of time until you will act really confident without even thinking about it. In other words, you'll be a natural. If on the other hand, you program it for failure, your unconscious mind will not stop until you act and become a failure. The choice is yours.

With that, you can now see why the unconscious mind is revered as a deity when it comes to lasting personal success in any given area of life. It's the puppet master behind our consistent habits and thinking.

Having said that, can you see now why external changes like habits, won't be successful unless your mind changes? Until you change your unconscious belief about yourself, you won't be able to experience true success. You'll go back to old habits and behaviors as soon as you "relax" yourself because your unconscious mind is your true nature.

So how do you actually change your mind, in particular your unconscious mind? Well, that's why God gave you your conscious mind. Remember how it functions as your unconscious mind's gatekeeper?

The primary mental strategy for building up your self-confidence is by consciously filtering what is passed on to your unconscious mind. You're actually doing it already, though you're just – sorry for the pun – unconsciously doing it. When you watch TV, listen or sing along to your favorite shows or read an article, you're actually sifting information. Some of it gets to through, some are filtered in the conscious mind.

Exposure

One of the ways you allow external factors like your environment, your relationships and experiences to shape your beliefs in the unconscious mind is through constant exposure. Ever wondered why you feel angry and hyper when you listen to heavy metal songs the whole day for 1 whole week? Or ever wondered why people who regularly attend church tend to memorize bible verses by heart even if they don't try hard? Or have you ever wondered why followers of certain celebrities tend to give off vibes that are reminiscent of the celebrities they're following? That's right, exposure. More is caught than taught.

By simply exposing yourself regularly to certain factors, those are able to enter your unconscious mind and over time, manifest naturally in your behavior and speech. By exposing yourself to factors that will build up your confidence, you become even more confident. This is why apprenticeships are very valuable. You learn much and deeply simply by exposing yourself to catch a master's impartations naturally.

Self-Talk

Talking to yourself doesn't exactly make you loonies, bro. Especially if you talk to yourself in a good way and that you are aware that you are talking to yourself! One way of talking right to yourself is through positive affirmations. Positive affirmations are – in layman's terms – good things you say to yourself over and over again with the intention of making those good things manifest in your life.

The first step in utilizing positive affirmations is to list things down. Take piece of paper and fold it lengthwise in half. On the right side, list down all your mindsets about why you're not confident such as:

-I'm not good enough;

-I don't have what it takes to be successful with women;

-I'm wuss;

-This is who I am for life and I can't change that;

-I can only be confident about myself when I become rich or accomplished; and

-Women won't ever find me attractive.

On the left side, list down the positive statements you want to replace those at the left, such as:

-I have what it takes;

-I can successfully attract and seduce women without having to pay them;

-I can be a cool and confident guy;

-I can change; and

-Women will find me attractive soon enough.

When you're done, tear the paper right down the middle and throw away the half that contains the negative mindsets that you have. On the other hand, keep and reproduce the one that contains all the positive affirmations. Post copies around your home, particularly the spots that you regularly hang out in – even the bathroom. Every time you see the list (exposure) anywhere in your home, read it aloud. As you hear yourself repeating those positive affirmations regularly, your unconscious mind will eventually pick up on it and before you know it, it'll start living it out through you without you even trying or noticing. You're gonna be a natural.

Just keep in mind that you should be relaxed as you read them, aloud or otherwise. Why? Trying too hard will hamper the affirmations' travel into your unconscious mind. How's this so? Remember that masterful execution of movements is done by the unconscious mind and as such, it needs to be able to operate freely. The moment you think and try so hard to make it work by memorizing it, among others, you hamper the work of your unconscious mind. It's like trying to cut the hair of your hyperactive 2 year-old or trying to "help" the lifeguard in rescuing you to shore. Just do it in a relaxed manner for optimal results. The moment you try to think about trying harder, don't.

Positive affirmations, once already acquired by your unconscious mind as official "targets", will be automatically executed or manifested by your unconscious mind. That doesn't mean however, your conscious mind gatekeeping activities should stop. Hell no! I highly suggest you continue with the practice so that there's no way in hell that wrong or negative mindsets can slip in. Just continue doing it in a relaxed way and you'll do great!

Oh, another thing about listing down your negative or wrong confidence mindsets, more than 1 heads are definitely better than just one. What I mean is if you have the benefit of getting feedback from the people you trust the most and are closest to, use it by asking them for their inputs. And because we all have blind spots, asking for the help or opinions of such people will help you minimize or identify all of them. You can only correct wrong beliefs and mindsets that you're aware of. They can also give you the benefit of being able to catch yourself if you're reverting back to your old, un-confident ways. Better nip it in the bud than to uproot the whole tree.

Positivity

Positivity is a way of viewing life or your experiences through an optimistic point of view. Let's consider the example of your alarm not going off at the time you set it because its battery died during the evening. There are 3 ways of looking at what just happened.

One way is to focus on the negative side – its consequences. You can dwell on the fact that you will be late for work and that possibly, you won't hear the end of it again from your grumpy supervisor. And you're not crazy to assume that especially if it's not the first time you were late to work.

Another way is to be indifferent about it. "I'll be late...so what? Everybody comes to work late every once in a while. Why should it be different with me?" you might think to yourself. While this approach is better than the negatron one, it's not the best. There's something much better.

The last approach is to focus on the bright side. You may consider the fact that by being late, you avoided getting into a serious accident had you left for work on time.

Now let's look at this from the perspective of going for the win, a.k.a. getting the digits of that hot girl you spotted in the bar and if it's your lucky night, go home with her. You approach this sweet, hot momma and begin small talk and employing your eye contacts. When you ask for her digits, she declines and asked to be excused, leaving you alone with two shot beer bottles on the counter. How should you process this?

You can take it negatively and think that you're a hopeless case, that you're ugly or worse, eye contact training sucks! Yeah, suck it in, boy, suck it in! You come back to your group's table with your tail in between your legs, your eyes sweaty like it ran a full marathon and moping the whole evening, ruining even the night of your friends.

You can just be indifferent and think nothing of it. Right, no biggie here – it's the way things normally go so I'm cool, y'all. You go back to your group's table and just learn nothing. By doing that, you'll probably make the same mistake next time and eventually, you'll be a pessimist.

Or you can be positive about it and think that by discovering another wrong way to approach a random hot woman in a bar, you lessen the number of future mistakes you'll potentially commit. This means you're 1 step closer to successfully getting a hot, random woman's digits and potentially going home with her! You go back to your table in still in high spirits and will be able to do thing better the next time you take another babe digit-scoring attempt. Compared to being indifferent, being positive helps you learn valuable lessons from "mistakes", be encouraged in the face of such mistakes and carry on until you finally succeed.

It's worth noting that positivity doesn't mean denying reality or being a Pollyanna. It simply means choosing to focus more on the bright side, actual or otherwise. Focusing more implies you also acknowledge the reality of the failed attempts. You just don't sulk in them or give it much weight than is required.

Remember, you can't right a wrong that you don't acknowledge as one. With positivity, you acknowledge that something went wrong but focus more on the positive aspect of that "wrong".

Self-Confidence Quick Hits

"The secret to getting ahead is getting started." – Mark Twain

Truth is, we all need a good way to get started on important new things we're trying to learn, like self-confidence. That's what this chapter is for – quick and practical ways to boost your self-confidence to help you hit the ground running and encourage you to continue developing it.

Try remembering something that you did really well, especially those that you did on the first try. When you mentally recall or recreate the feelings and sensations associated with past successes, you enjoy a dose of a feel-good chemical called dopamine in your brain, helping you feel confident right off the bat.

Indulging in something you're very good at is another quick and practical way of boosting self-confidence. This is a very real reminder that you are indeed capable and in control. Personally,

I like to play the guitar, especially Skid Row's I Remember You. It never fails to give me a good rush of dopamine.

A relatively long list of pending items can be a potent self-confidence buster. So what are you waiting for dude? Finish off that freakin' list now! More than just being able to breathe a sigh of relief, getting things done helps you actually accomplish things and as you know, accomplishments help boost self-confidence.

Being thankful for what you have can be a very good self-confidence quick boost. How can you genuinely do that? By thinking of other people who are less fortunate than you, e.g., people who don't have a home or don't eat 3 times a day due to poverty. Sometimes, having a different perspective is enough to boost self-confidence. That happened to me once, when I volunteered to build houses for a poor community. Prior to that, I felt like crap believing I'm missing out a lot in life, which made me feel insecure about myself. But after staying in the community for several days to build humble houses that meant a lot to the poor people in that community, I got to experience losing what I have without actually losing them. It shifted my perspective from focusing on what I don't have to what I do have, which addressed my feelings of insecurity.

Do something you really, really love like sleeping the whole day, enjoying reruns of your favorite TV shows or shoot hoops – whatever gives you a feeling of refreshment and rest. In today's fast-paced society, you can get too busy and highly strung due and indulging in your favorite activities becomes scarce. The more often you feel refreshed and rested, the less critical you can be of yourself and be more confident and relaxed.

Indulging on your favorite food and drinks every now and then is a great way to boost self-confidence quickly. While it's true that health is wealth, there is such a thing as eating "too healthy", which robs you of your joy and spunk! And because eating healthy is often equated to rapid weight loss, i.e. crash and highly restrictive diets, it has the tendency to increase stress and sensitivity as well as risks for deadly rebounds of binge eating and ultimately, more weight. Moderate indulgence in your favorite treats makes long-term healthy eating more palatable, bearable and sustainable. Talk about quick and long-term confidence boost, eh?

Going for a run, a bike ride or just about any fun aerobic exercise helps release another feel-good chemical in your brain – endorphins. This is what's responsible for what's called runners' high (or bikers' high or just about any high experienced from enjoyable sustained exercise). Personally, going for a run or bike ride never fails to help boost my mood and my self-confidence.

A big chunk of feeling confident is about looking good. As such, buying new clothes can be a good self-confidence quick hit. To maximize the self-confidence raising effect of your budget, bring along someone who has an eye for fashion to help you pick the clothes look best on you. For this, I highly recommend bringing along a female friend who has excellent taste. After all, you wanna be confident around the hot ladies, right?

Eye Contact And Attraction

"Looking into someone's eyes changes the entire conversation."
– Kushandwizdom on Pinterest

Eyes are often referred to as the windows of one's soul. As such, it can also be one of your best weapons for attracting and seducing the women of your choice. Looking deeply into your woman's eyes whenever you talk to or smile at her can help unleash the amazing attraction and seductive powers of your eyes enough to make her remember you. Looking for a while at the woman you fancy will help send her the message that you're game and confident and not afraid of her. Remember about confidence, bro?

ATTRACTION

Sizzling eye contact is a good barometer of the attraction present between you and a woman. Regardless if you're in a crowded pub, across the street or on the opposite side of the room, eye contact is often times your first contact point with a woman, which could lead to something more if you play your cards right.

You can use your eyes to tell her that you're attracted to her using an unwavering, confident and friendly eye contact. Use it well like Luke Skywalker uses his light saber and your dating life will be much more colorful and exciting.

Speaking of eye contact, this is the part where you'll actually have to take off your sunglasses, no matter how expensive and chic they are. Otherwise, how can your eyes do the talking? It's like trying to talk to another person on the opposite side of a police interrogation room's one-sided mirror. If you've built your self-confidence to a healthy enough level, you won't hesitate to remove your sunglasses. In fact, you'll even be excited to let your eyes do the talking and remove them a.s.a.p!

Direct and intense eye contact is something that many women find attractive in men. Possibly it's because most men are afraid to give such eye contact especially if the woman is gorgeously hot. A man who's able to do that sends a subtle message to a woman that he's not like most men who are scared of them – he's alpha.

Although eye contact can be a very powerful attraction and seduction tool, it works best in conjunction with other tactics like body language and voice control. The sum of the parts can definitely be greater than the whole, dude! We'll talk about body language too in order to maximize your eye contact results.

HOW MUCH IS ENOUGH

I wish there's something like a table of elements of multiplication table that can give an objective benchmark by which you can determine if your eye contact is too much or too little but unfortunately, there's none. The good news however, is that there are factors you against which you can evaluate if the eye contact you're giving another person is appropriate or not.

Conversation Topic

It's not by random chance that professional counselors and shrinks' couches are arranged in such a way as to minimize eye contact between them and their counselees or patients.

Why? Because most – if not all – of the time, the topics discussed are very shameful or embarrassing. I mean, why else would they seek professional help if their concerns were as serious as having to decide between getting an iPhone 6 or Samsung Galaxy S6 for their birthday gift.

On the other hand, why is it that most restaurants frequented by lovers feature smaller than usual tables, huh? That's right –

intimacy. The topics of conversation between lovers are so intimate as to require paying more attention via eye contact. And the eye contact duration is much longer too between people who are either in love or in lust as compared to shrinks and their patients again, due to the topics of their conversations.

Proximity

Have you ever noticed how people talk in elevators? In particular, noticed the amount of eye contact? Not much huh? It's because the relatively small space makes people too close to each other for extended eye contact, if any. At such proximity, it can be quite strenuous on the eyes to establish and maintain the same amount of eye contact as when outside the elevator.

Attention Required

There are situations when more attention is required. When giving instructions of talking, people usually look at the other person around 75% of the time while if they're on the receiving end (listening), they look at the other person around 40% of the time.

Nature Of Conversation

The more serious is the nature of the conversation, the longer or more eye contact is usually given. For example, a doctor who is talking to a patient about his serious medical condition hardly breaks eye contact. If the conversation is more about cooperation than competition, eye contact is also generally more. Lastly, if the conversation is about trying to convince the other party to agree, the persuading party tends to look at the person being persuaded more.

Relationship

Generally speaking, we all tend to look more at people we like compared to those who we don't. In fact, our pupils dilate when looking at people we like - or women who turn us on. The amount of eye contact can also indicate who between the parties is the dominant one and can signal a threat.

Ethnicity

People's cultural backgrounds can also influence the amount of eye contact they're comfortable both giving and receiving. For example, European cultures tend to have less eye contact compared to near East cultures. In some religiously conservative countries, looking at women who aren't your wives are frowned upon and can get you into trouble.

Robert Moore

Why A High Status Eye Contact Is So Important

Unless you've been living under a rock, you should know that material things lie.

Supercars lie, houses lie, shiny stuff lie.

Men lie, women lie.

But remember this: it is IMPOSSIBLE for the eyes to lie.

They just can't do that. They will reveal every part of your soul, even that one part you're trying to hide.

Even if you are brilliant, even if you have a powerful, commanding body language along with a deep, clear, strong voice... people (especially women) could still not trust you.

But they CAN'T not trust your eyes. They are the truest signal of power, high-status and leadership.

A deep, relaxed eye contact SCREAMS high-status, louder than anything else.

That's why it's so important for your success in life, with women, in your job. Smart women will consciously look at the eyes of a man, especially in situations of high pressure, because they want to see if he can handle the tension.

Picture in your mind this scene: two individuals are socially interacting and as they're talking and looking at each other's eyes, some sort of tension is being built; she can handle it, the man can't.

What happens? Obviously, the man loses, and she will not forget that.

But if he can handle the high pressure with a strong, relaxed eye contact, then that's a representation of pure POWER. And she will notice that for sure, besides being overwhelmed by a strong sexual attraction for him.

In fact, if a man can't even handle that type of eye contact in a public situation, maybe while just having a normal conversation with her, then what is she going to think about the way that he's going to fu*k her?

He can't even look in her eyes while talking! How is he supposed to look at her while having sex?

The desire of every woman is to look at your eyes and see a powerful, confident, alpha man.

You must tell them, through your eyes, that you're going to fu*k them like a god.

That's what she wants to see. That's what your eyes, if used correctly, are going to tell her in a direct, smooth and subconscious way.

So, don't be that weak guy who can't even look at her in a public setting. You learned how important your inner game is in order to become truly confident.

Now, do yourself a favor: go through this training, do the exercises, follow my tips and then you'll be free to go out there attracting any woman you want.

Rapport

When you and that chick you're very much into are getting along very well or are hitting it off, then you have rapport. Rapport is very, very important if you want to attract the ladies and bring 'em home. Why?

Developing rapport is very critical to your seduction success. She may feel comfy with you while you talk all night but comfy is several levels below attraction, dude. Comfy is like the welcome mat to your house of love! If you don't really connect on a much deeper level, your seduction operation is doomed.

So how does eye contact establish rapport? For one, it can make the chick you're talking to feel like she's very special and that you really are interested in what she has to say. Don't you feel the same way with people who look at you when you're talking?

Listening isn't just done with the ears...it's also done with the eyes.

In fact, listening to the other person without looking at them is pretty much the same as not listening at all! Some of the women I've hooked up with in the past would complain that I'm not listening to them even if I am able to repeat what they just said verbatim. Why? It's because I wasn't looking. They'd say, "Are you even listening? Why aren't you looking at me?"

If you've ever experienced that yourself, then you know the seemingly mystical powers of eye contact when it comes to establishing rapport. In fact, it may seem that without eye contact, there can be no rapport. Unless of course one or both of your are blind. That's another story.

One of the most famous people in the world is Bill Clinton. He's not as hot looking as Brad Pitt or Bradley Cooper nor is he as rich as Tom Cruise. But he sure has a way with the ladies, if you know what I'm talking about. It's been said that one of his most potent weapons of charisma – and possibly seduction – is his eyes. His ability to use eye contact seems to be the stuff legends are made of.

Dig this: most people who swear by his charisma say that the way he looks at you is as if you're the only person in the room – that you're special. And one of the basic principles in human psychology is that people like people who like them or are genuinely interested in them. Eye contact, if done properly, has that magical ability to make people believe that you are genuinely into them.

N' Sync

No, I'm not talkin' about J.T. (Justin Timberlake) here, dude. When you and the other person are so into the groove that the two of you are able to communicate so easily, the two of you are said to be in sync. How does this look like? She laughs at most of your jokes that most of your friends find to be either too corny or too intellectual to grasp. You're able finish each other's sentences as if you two have known each other for years now. Being in sync is another critical characteristic of attraction and seduction. And your ability to properly utilize eye contact can go a long way towards helping you achieve this state with the other person.

How does being in sync totally look like? The best picture I can think of are professional dance partners, ala Dancing With The Stars. When you see them execute those very complicated moves, you wonder what would happen if one of them becomes off sync even for just a split second, especially if the move involved some jumping and catching on the part of the guy. But when you look at it, you have to admit those dance partners are just amazing to watch. It makes you think that it is possible for two very different minded people to come together and work fluidly as one.

So how does proper eye contact help get you in sync with that hot chick you're after? There's a principle in psychology called mirroring. As the name suggests, it involves imitating the other person's gestures, which unconsciously makes her feel connected with you. There are many different ways synchrony – or the state of being in sync – can be achieved. In bigger events like a pep rally or a stand up comedy routine, body language is the primary way of achieving synchrony. But in more intimate settings – like when you're alone talking to her – it's the eyes that do it, with proper eye contact of course.

On the flip side, this is one reason why I don't look at the eyes of pesky and persistent salespeople. Why? It's because from experience, once they're able to establish eye contact, or at least long enough to make a difference, I end up being convinced to buy something I often times regret buying. Such is the power of proper eye contact. Can you imagine harnessing that power to get under the pants of a very hot woman?

Intentions

In the seduction game, intentions do matter. At least the timing does. If women immediately sense that you're only goal is to bang them, say goodbye to your seduction and attraction attempts. You're already dead in the water even before you begin.

That being said, your eyes can either help you communicate your intention in the best possible way or make you come off as a maniac right off the bat. Why? It's because your eyes say a lot about you. Every wondered why these popular lines from popular songs tell what they do:

-"Look into my eyes, you will see just how much you mean to me." – (Everything I Do) I Do It For You by Bryan Adams

-"Looking through the eyes of love." – Through The Eyes Of Love by Melissa Manchester

-"When I look into your eyes, I can see how much I love you and it makes me realize." – When I Look Into Your Eyes by Firehouse

-"In your eyes, I can see the reason why our love's alive...in your eyes." – In Your Eyes by George Benson

Yesiree...your eyes tell a lot about what you plan to do and how to do it.

How You Should NOT Make Eye Contact

"Private eyes – clap clap – they're watching you – clap clap – they see your every move." – Hall And Oates, Private Eyes

Not all kinds of eye contact will help you win women over. To this extent, it's worth explaining that not all eye contact is seductive. Many of them are downright creepy and will make women jump into a smoldering cauldron of molten steel.

STARING

One of them is staring, which is basically looking at a person for in the eye for say, about 3 hours straight with eyes wide open. Creepy huh? Told ya.

Many men don't seem to get the difference between staring and a healthy dose of eye contact. They hardly feel that they're staring rather than giving their utmost attention to a woman they're talking to. Well, it's because they can't see themselves do it. To this extent, it'd be wise to ask for your friends' opinion if you have the tendency to stare. You can also ask some of the girls you scared off before if you stare.

EYE-GROPING

Another wrong form of eye contact is eye groping, which is staring at someone without his or her consent. Let's put it this way: how would you feel if you know that someone is watching you, whether they're people or ghosts. Either way, it's creepy right?

Now, imagine you're a girl with a really gorgeous face and a hot body. You're wearing your teenie weenies at the gym and you catch this obese, slobby and maniac-looking hulk of a man eye-groping you. Now, is that seductive? I don't think so. If it was probably Jake Gyllenhaal, you'd be turned on. But men like him who can get away with it are far and few in between and you're probably not one of them.

To give you an idea if you're eye groping or not, ask yourself if you have ever stared at a sexy woman's boobs while she did the peck deck machine at the gym and she doesn't know it? That'd be eye groping. How do you think she'd respond if she finds out you're doing that? Unless she's an exhibitionist nymph, I'd say you'd be kicked out of the gym.

What Is A High Status Eye Contact?

So, what exactly is a high status eye contact?

High-status eye contact is the complete control of your own eyes and attention. You will look where you want, when you want, for how long you want, unaffected by anything external, while remaining aware of social norms and influence.

External things won't affect you: wherever you're looking, is entirely where YOU want to be looking.

I want you to become totally non-reactive to external things and events.

For example, if you're looking at a girl that you like and she suddenly turns and notices that you're looking at her, you won't look away. You will keep looking at her eyes, in a relaxed and powerful way, and then look away when you'll want to do so, with smooth and slow movements.

But, as you read in the previous chapters, always remember to be aware of social norms: I don't want you to stare every person as a weird psychopath.

You can hold your eye contact for a couple seconds and appreciate what you're seeing: that's fine, you're a high status male and you can do that.

Just don't look at her eyes for one minute straight thinking that it's a high status behavior, because in reality it isn't.

There is a threshold of being socially powerful to being socially weird. And looking for too long at someone will cross that threshold in just one second.

Never pass that threshold, always be aware of it!

Since you will look where you truly want to look, your attention will become more valuable. Every person, male or female, will have to work harder for your attention and things will have to be better in order to gain your look. That's something that every badass male has in common: they're not wasting their time looking at something they're not really interested in, because their focus is only on their mission, their path to success.

This was an introduction for the #1 big, badass rule of eye contact:

When YOU are talking to someone, you will look at the eyes of the other person for about the 90% of the time: the remaining 10%, just look at the distance, painting your vision and organizing your thoughts.

On the other hand, when THEY are talking to you, you will look at them for about the 50-60% of the time.

So, when you're talking, I want you to PIERCE their soul with your eye contact: be confident and strong, you can do hold it as long as you want, because you're a real badass! Looking at their eyes while you're talking gives you authority and commands their respect and attention.

Remember to keep breathing: if you forget to do so, you won't be able to keep that pressure for so long.

Literally, breathe that tension deeply, and push it out from your body with a long expiration.

A rigid jaw also causes a lot of tension in your face: relax your jaw muscles by opening your mouth wide and breathing deeply. You can also massage these muscles if you want to, it'll be helpful and you'll relieve some stress.

When they are talking to you, slowly look away, then back to their eyes, then again slowly look away. Keep making them fighting for your valuable attention: they'll have to work harder and harder because you'll be a high status badass, who looks where he wants, when he wants.

Remember that your head turns must be SLOW: a secret law of body language says that the person who turns his head the least is perceived as the higher status one.

We'll cover that now, don't worry badass.

Powerful Eye Contact: Tips and Tricks

So, you now understand what a high status eye contact is and why it's so important.

Before we get to the practical exercises, I want to share with you some tips and tricks, which will make your eye contact more powerful and your perceived value even higher.

As you read in the last chapter, your head movements will be SLOW.

If you are used to turn your head left and right very quickly right now, BANISH this low status behavior from your life.

From now on, when you'll turn your head, it must seem like it doesn't move.

In reality, it does move slowly, but your eyes are doing the main job of focusing on another thing.

So, take your time when moving your head.

Learn to keep your head more still.

PRO TIP #1: The Person Who Moves The Head The Least Is Usually Perceived As The Higher Status Person.

Practice and focus on making this little change in your behavior and you'll be rewarded. A lot!

Now, I'm going to share with you another little tip, because value never ends.

When you really, really like something, your eyes will literally open up a little bigger than normal, simply because you want to take more of what you're looking at in. If you're looking at a fantastic view, maybe at the Coliseum or at the Niagara Falls, that's not a low status behavior, it's just cool and normal.

But if you're looking at the eyes of a woman, then squint your eyes a little.

If you notice, that's a typical trait of George Clooney. And you probably know what women think about him...

Basically, with the little squinting of your eyes, you're telling her that you don't want to take that much of her in.

Your eyes are saying: "I don't like you that much", "I'm not sure about you...", therefore creating all kinds of sexual attraction in her mind, because you're pushing yourself away from her.

Look at these pictures right here and notice how they're squinting their eyes a little bit:

Their smirk is always there, but they're literally breaking rapport with their eyes. As you may have read in my book *Voice Training*, the person who breaks rapport is often times the higher status one.

If you haven't, don't lose this opportunity. Go get this game-changing information on Amazon.com.

You can also play with this trick the other way around.

Since our eyes get bigger when we see something that we like, our pupils will also dilate and get bigger, because, again, we just want more of it.

So, when you're talking to a girl and you feel she's into you, just look at her pupils real quick. If they are dilated and bigger than normal, she obviously likes what she's seeing and what she's hearing.

Always be aware of the ambient lighting changes! But if the lighting remains the same, and the pupils are dilated, then... good job, bro.

PRO TIP #2: Initiate, Don't Retaliate

Remember how we talked about pushing her attraction buttons with confidence?

Another way you can use eye contact to communicate that is by initiating eye contact with her. What you're saying to her by doing so is you're confident unlike most men who are afraid to do so and that you're the leader, not the follower, in whatever relationship may already be there between you and her. Remember how women want their men to be in control?

It's worth noting that most women won't offer to initiate eye contact. And with the scarcity of confident men who are willing to take risks and the lead in relationships, initiating eye contact will be a great way to start your potentially sexual relationship with her.

This is why I emphasized the importance of building up your self-confidence or inner game even before learning and applying eye contact techniques. You won't be able to break the ice and initiate if your inner game sucks.

If you feel you're not yet that confident or if your inner game is still weak, go back to the first few chapters on confidence and attraction.

PRO TIP #3: Start From The Eyes And Move To The Lips

If you'd like to make her feel horny, this is one of the best ways to use eye contact. While talking to her, maintain a relatively hardcore look in her eyes, much like how a laser pointer focuses on a main point on the projector screen. Then move your gaze to her lips. Wait for a few seconds, then return your gaze back to her eyes.

Eyes, lips, eyes, lips – repeat as needed. As you look at her lips, imagine all those things that she can do with your body using those wet lips. I know, can you imagine her giving you head? Nice.

At that point, I sense you're already starting to be aroused. That's good because that's the message you want to subtly send her using your eyes.

Believe me, the hornier you are, the stronger the message of arousal you'll send her through your eyes. Just be aware of the duration ok? You don't want to come of as some desperate sex maniac. Just continue keeping your calm and confident composure while communicating with your eyes all those nasty thoughts you're having of her lips on your body – or body part. By the time the conversation is over, she'll probably be wet where it shouldn't be. And it ain't her underarms, dawg!

PRO TIP #4: Gaze Longer

Also known as extended gaze, this eye contact flirting style is all about making her just a bit uncomfortable but not too much.

Uncomfortable enough to know you're not like other emasculated men but not too uncomfortable to bunch you together with the stalkers and psychopaths.

While you're talking to a woman, extend the duration of your look or gaze for a bit longer than you usually would. To make you more of a seducer than a stalker, accompany the extended gaze with warm in your eyes or a small smile. To make it even better, adapt a relatively relaxed or easy body posture and tilt your neck slightly.

PRO TIP #5: Peek A Boo

In contrast to pro tip #4, this one involves brief and short glances, which are more subtle and demure than an extended gaze. The beautiful thing about peeking is that it's sly while at the same time noticeable. If the extended gaze is more about confidence and control, the peek-a-boo is more about excitement. She'll be confused: "Is he really looking at me? If so, why? Do I look funny? Is he attracted to me? Or is he looking at someone else and I just happen to be in his line of sight? Dammit, I need to know!"

Such "confusion" – if you play it right – can become uncontainable excitement. The more excited she becomes, the more open she will be to your attempts at flirting and hopefully, getting into her pants.

PRO TIP #6 Full Body Scan

This can be quite a tricky tip and a potentially high risk high reward one because compared to the others, this one's more sensual and relatively brazen. It's a hit or miss kind of thing. If she's game, she may respond similarly. If not, she may never look at you again.

The full body scan is an extension of the extended gaze. After an extended gaze, you switch to looking at her lips for a longer-than-usual period, followed by the same to her bosom, legs and back up to her eyes.

PRO TIP #7: Mix It Up

The more variety you employ, the more unpredictable you become. The more unpredictable you become, the more exciting you are to her. The more excited she is about you...you know where I'm going with this, don't ya boy?

Mixing it up makes it fun and exciting for you too. I don't know about you but I find it fun and exciting that I never know what particular eye contact technique will push her buttons or amplify the attraction already present. The constant mixing up keeps things fresh and exciting, which I am able to transmit to her.

PRO TIP #8: Use The Appropriate Body Language

Remember how I said that eye contact works best in conjunction with body language and voice control? Guess what, it's not just any body language. It has to be appropriate.

It's best to illustrate some inappropriate body languages to avoid so you can clearly get the picture. One body language to avoid while flirting, attracting and seducing using eye contact is rubbing your lips with your tongue. Ewweee, nothing else reeks of dirty old man (DOM) than that. Put yourself in the shoes of a woman just for a second. Imagine a man Pro Tip #3 while rubbing his lips with his tongue. Would you be turned on or off by it? I rest my case.

Another example would be standing in a slouched position with your crotch practically pointing at her while employing the full-body scan. That would be so obviously creepy. That can also land you in jail.

Other similar body languages to avoid include rubbing your groin area, miming and pointing out her body parts. For more ideas on how not to act while employing eye contact flirting, check out The Big Bang Theory's Howard Wolowitz's smooth and suave (not!) body language. Later on, I'll teach you some of the best body language movements to help amplify your eye contact techniques' attraction and seduction powers.

PRO TIP #9: Group Talk

Joining a group discussion or study can help you improve your eye contact skills for attraction and seduction. How? It's like those ankle weights used to increase one's vertical leap. A person wears those weights as he jogs, plays ball or simply walks around, the idea being is to train the legs to get used to heavier weight so that when he removes it and enters a real game, he jumps significantly higher.

In the context of eye contact, talking to a group regularly forces you to practice eye contact on more people. In particular, what you'll get to practice are not the seduction and attraction techniques but your confidence in looking people in the eye. When you become used to the "heavier" load of making eye contact with numerous people at a time, doing so with just one person can be much easier for you.

PRO TIP #10: Practice, Practice And More Practice

Mastering eye contact techniques for attracting and seducing women, just as with all other endeavors worthy of mastering, requires much practice. It's been cited in Malcolm Gladwell's bestselling book Outliers that it takes on average about 10,000 hours of practice to truly master something. Now, there have been various reactions to this claim that Malcolm Gladwell only cited from the work of a well-known scientist but the point is simple: the more you practice, the better you get at something. Practice makes excellent.

The thing with practice is that you don't rush both the practice session and its fruits. Successfully practicing the art of eye contact attraction and seduction requires dedication and is best done in baby steps. Otherwise, you might be overwhelmed with too much too do and be disappointed if you don't immediately enjoy the fruits. Think of this as a medium to long term project with long term benefits.

PRO TIP #10: Raise The Brows

Raising your eyebrows can also help you raise the likelihood of being able to make a great first impression with the woman you want to seduce. In fact, you may just not be aware of it but you are already doing it to the people you already know and are comfortable with.

An eyebrow flash is when you raise your eyebrows for less than a second at a person you want to attract. According to Dr. Kate Fox of the Social Issues Research Center in London, doing this makes the person you want to attract think that you must be an acquaintance that she may have just forgotten or doesn't recognize. As you begin your approach, she may already be starting to recall who the hell you are. You can take advantage of this "confusion" by initiating conversation about where the two of you may have possibly met. Just make sure you stay clear of the old cliché "Do I know you from somewhere?" crap, right?

Now that you know these little tricks, it's time to really train your eye contact and your ability to keep tension, no matter what happens or who you are with.

Robert Moore

Eye Contact Training: The Exercises

We're going to train your eye contact in two different ways.

First, you're going to train it from the outside in, for ATTENTION purposes.

You will use different techniques in order to make your attention more valuable and make other people work harder for it.

Then, you're going to train it from the inside out, for TENSION purposes.

You will practice different exercises in order to handle stressful situations from the inside, so that your eyes will clearly show that you have no problem with keeping tension, no matter the circumstances.

So, let's start!

ATTENTION TRAINING TECHNIQUES

As discussed, remember **the 90/60 rule**.

When you're talking to someone, look at their eyes, maybe with a little squint going on, for the 90% of the time. When they're talking to you, look at them for the 60%; be present, listen to them, but move your eyes slowly to somewhere else. They will have your present energy, but they won't have your full attention. This will create a space for them to fight for your attention and for your approval, especially when talking to girls. That's a powerful, high status trait that is always perceived on a subconscious level.

The slow turn.

The movement of the head is usually a great honest signal of status for other people. A high status person does not jerk his head fast, turning a lot in different directions. His head does not move as much: it tends to stay still. When it moves, its movement is slow, smooth, relaxed, controlled.

Practice it consciously and it will become automatic in just a few days.

If someone calls your name, don't turn right away; wait a second and then start turning your head slowly: that's a true signal of power.

The still head.

As discussed, you head will be more still. You will notice that people will look at you as a high status person and it will become really obvious to others.

When you want to look somewhere else, you don't necessarily move your head, you just move your eyes slowly from one point to another.

Remember this:

How you look away says everything.

Remember this sentence while you're training your attention.

For example, if you're making some eye contact with a girl, you don't turn your head away quickly and jerky. That would communicate low status.

But if you look away from her slowly and like there's something more interesting for you to look at... she, all of a sudden, is already chasing your approval and attention. She gets the FEELING that you're a high status, dominant guy, who does not need a hot girl in his life, because he's already in an abundance state.

TENSION TRAINING TECHNIQUES

The singular focus exercise.

That's what you're going to do: 3 times in the morning, after your shower or whatever, turn your TV on (or PC, or laptop). On its top, put any tiny object that you can look at. Play a video, or a film, whatever you can watch, with the sound off.

You're going to stare directly at that tiny thing, that little spot.

Be calm, relaxed and focused on it.

Hold that for about 60 seconds. During that time, you will notice that your focus will go away. When it happens, don't judge it and keep going. Just recognize it and calmly get back to the little spot.

You'll start to feel tension in your body. That's cool: breathe deeply and stay relaxed.

After the 60 seconds, relax and take a break. Pause for about a minute and then do it again for a total of 3 sets, 60 seconds each.

When you become really good at this, turn the volume on and keep your focus on the tiny object.

If you do this for about 2 weeks, you'll notice that your ability to look someone in the eyes will drastically improve.

Holding tension will become a breeze for you.

The cold shower exercise.

It's similar to the first one, but it will increase your ability to hold eye contact during stressful or painful situations.

When you go in the shower, make it hot for a little bit, so that you can warm up. Then turn it cold for 60 seconds and make it hit your whole body, your neck in particular, because it's the most sensitive area.

This is going to hit you, it's a lot of physical tension.

That's important because, in terms of energy, physical tension equals emotional tension. If you can resist the former, you will also resist the latter.

To perform this exercise, look at a little spot somewhere in your shower while the cold water is hitting you. Keep your facial muscles relaxed and stay calm; breathe deeply and don't start to move or scream.

Stare at that spot for about 60 seconds and then turn the water hot again and relax.

Then go cold again for a total of 3 sets, 60 seconds each.

This exercise is so powerful because when you're dealing with a hot girl that you like, you'll probably be a little nervous. Everyone feels something in those situations, even the most expert dating coach. But, at least to her, you will look like you have no problem holding that tension. Or, even if you are feeling the tension, you're just cool with it because you've experienced worse situations... in your shower.

The ability of remaining cool, calm and collected during stressful situations is ALWAYS a signal of pure, powerful, high status.

The "get caught" exercise.

As soon as you finish reading this book, I want you to stare at the eyes of 5 people.

During lunch, in subway, wherever you have the chance to do so.

Look directly at their eyes, get caught, and keep looking for other 3 seconds. Breathe deeply and stay relaxed. Think about how great you are, how powerful is your high status while you're staring at them.

Fill your head with positive thoughts and loop them all the time.

Then, slowly turn your head away, as you learned before, and leave them with the feeling of being stared from a badass alpha male.

Do not stare too much, three seconds is okay. I don't want you to go to jail.

But remember, the most important exercise is **CONSTANT PRACTICE**. If you really want to master the art of eye contact, keep practicing it every time you can. With girls, with your boss, with strangers. Practice excellence. Always.

And five years from now, just imagine how great of a master you'll be. Eye contact is a skill, just like any other nonverbal communication technique. And as a skill, it can be mastered and WILL be mastered.

OWN IT!

Robert Moore

Move Your Body

"My father taught me things about body language that psychologists have been catching up with ever since. He always knew when I was lying, because my posture was all wrong." – Richard Griffiths

The power of eye contact can be greatly enhanced or complemented with the right body language. It's been said that in terms of effective communications, only 10% to 20% is verbal and the rest is non-verbal or body language.

That's how significant body language is. In fact, other experts peg the percentage of effective communications that can be attributed to body language at 90%! That's both an exciting and a scary thought, don't you think so?

Just how important is body language to maximizing your eye contact techniques? You may correctly employ all the right eye contact techniques but if the rest of your body's out of sync, it'll all be for naught. Your eyes may scream alpha but your body whispers omega male. Your eyes may say sexy but your body language may indicate maniac.

Don't worry man, you don't need to pay attention to a million micro facial and body expressions here just to optimize and support your proper eye contact techniques. Just a coupe of postures, movements and gestures is enough. They may be few but they're certainly potent.

POSTURE

When people say posture, what normally comes to mind is standing up straight and erect. While good posture certainly does include those, being confident, attractive and alpha isn't just about that. It also means standing tall. But what does it mean to stand tall? Here's how:

-Start at the legs by straightening them at full extension and avoid looking lazy and bending.

-After the legs, pay attention to your spine. To stand tall means not hunching over or leaning forward. The ideal spine posture is one where your back looks something like a small "C". What this means is you puff your chest out a bit, stand upright and draw your shoulders back.

-Lastly, remember to exercise moderation here. Don't exaggerate your "C" position, puff your chest too far forward as if your being pulled hard or draw your shoulders too far back like they're gonna be ripped away from your torso. Too much of a good thing is still too much, bro!

FACIAL EXPRESSIONS

Your face, like your eyes, can also tell so many things about you.

As such, many studies and books have been conducted and written, respectively, on how to read it. In particular, I know when my girl's lying just by looking at her face. Women, being the more accurate species when it comes to reading facial expressions, can pick up a lot from your facial expressions – whether you're really confident or not and whether you're alpha or omega. As such, facial expressions can either be a very good supplement to or a bad saboteur of your eye contact techniques.

So what facial expressions can help you maximize your eye contact techniques for optimum charisma and expression of confidence and attraction?

-Eyes: Your eyes shouldn't look like those of a deer's who is about to be run down by a speeding bicycle in the middle of a midnight road, i.e. wide and open. It won't just contradict your eye contact techniques by making you look like you're surprised and unable to control the situation. It will also exaggerate your eye contact techniques' sexual innuendoes and make you look less like a hot stud and more of a maniac.

-Smile: Smiling is very crucial particularly when meeting a woman for the first time. Doing so isn't just about sending the message that you're open to anything – it's also about sending her the message that you're confident about yourself and in your ability to have everything, including her, under control. Master the art of smiling genuinely – especially with your eyes – and you'll significantly enhance your eye contact techniques' effectiveness.

-As with posture, make sure you don't overdo the smiling thing by smiling too wide and too frequently because by doing that, you change the message from "I'm confident and in control" to "I'm naïve and nice", which is totally omega.

HAND POSITION

Although not as potent a supplement to your eye contact techniques, it can still be a good way to reinforce them and the body language technique you want to employ.

Hands on your sides tell her that you're open, relaxed and confident while crossed hands scream close-mindedness, insecurity or God-forbid, opposition to her hotness or sexual innuendoes.

Hand in your pockets are neither alpha nor omega but will depend on your overall posture. If you're looking down and slouching, it says "I'm insecure and weak!" If standing tall and looking straight ahead, it can communicate confidence or being comfortable.

HEAD POSITION

The way you position your head also plays a great part in helping your eye contact techniques send the right message, sexual attraction, confidence and alpha male status. For example, keeping a straightforward head – one that's neither high nor low – says "I'm dominant, secure in who I am and confident."

On the other hand, looking down tells your lady that you're scared of people, not confident in who you are and you're shy. Looking high isn't good as well because you may implicitly say to her that you're arrogant or worse, innocent and unassuming.

THE WALK

The way you walk is probably the second biggest way you can communicate your alpha male status to the woman you're trying to hunt. Your strides can either confirm or deny the confidence and alpha male status you initially impressed upon your fair game of a woman. Long slow strides reflect confidence and control while short fast ones indicate that you're always in a hurry, which means you're either not in control, insecure or worse – both! Quick and short strides are appropriate only when you're late for a very important occasion.

OBSERVE

Another way to get a good idea of how facial expressions and body language can enhance your high status eye contact is by observing the alpha males in your immediate social circle. Or you can watch clips of James Bond on YouTube, particularly Pierce Brosnan's and Sean Connery's. I love the character of Harvey Specter from the TV show Suits. Remember, much is caught than taught.

Conclusion

You got it, badass.

You discovered why a high status eye contact is so powerful and I invite you to consider its potential in your business life, and in your social and sexual life.

If you commit yourself to improve it, using the exercises I provided to you, then your perceived value will skyrocket: that's a promise.

People will start doing things for you, because you'll become more influential.

They will look to you for decisions.

... and for the most part, they'll simply do whatever you say.

A high status, deep, relaxed Eye Contact is THAT powerful, because it commands attention and it's always perceived as a badass skill.

Unfortunately, it's not enough in certain situations.

Your value would be much, much higher if you could only associate a solid body language to your badass eyes.

Think about it: how great would it be for you to be recognized as a commanding LEADER?

People will look at your positioning and think... *"Damn, this guy must have power in his life"*. Then they will find a validation to their thought looking at your eyes. And they will be amazed by your ability to show dominance through two of the most honest signals of high status, BODY LANGUAGE and EYE CONTACT.

Body language is so important, that I decided to give you a free preview of my book *Body Language Training*.

A badass body positioning is so rare nowadays: only political leaders and famous actors know certain secrets that the sea of mediocrity is unaware of.

I will show you those secrets and teach you the exact method I followed in order to make my body language stand out and my walk incredibly attractive to women.

Don't lose this opportunity: you'll find it in the next chapter, so go ahead and read it.

Thank you again, my friend, and good luck!

Robert Moore

Robert Moore

Preview Of "Body Language Training"

The 10 Principles of High Status Body Language

Now I will show you different high status body language positions and principles.

First of all, understand that as a high status man, you will always make yourself comfortable first, wherever you go. That's not a selfish behavior, since it will give everyone else around you the permission to relax, feel good and be comfortable too.

#1 principle: take up more space.

Low status people tend to make themselves small, invisible, sitting or standing in an uncomfortable way. They are not sending their energy out to the world, because they don't see themselves as high status persons: in their mind they're not worth it.

They're closed on themselves, they're hiding from the outside world.

You, on the other hand, will think that your energy is so valuable that of course you're willing to share it with the world, so you're going to open yourself and take up more space.

Spread your legs and your arms: be comfortable!

Simply ask yourself: "am I closed or open right now?"

You'll know the answer: take action and open up the positioning of your body.

You may ask, why is that so? It's because shy and unconfident people are more concerned about what people will say. They're too afraid of "offending" people or getting really bad comments about them like they're insensitive, arrogant or being chutzpah-tic.

And if you were paying attention, you'll remember that these are the 3 common misconceptions about confidence that turn most men off from even the idea of becoming confident. This is a potent disease called "people pleasing".

Confident, alpha men aren't concerned with people's opinions and comments because they're sure of themselves. They do respect other people's opinions and beliefs and as such, they also respect their own. They're also able to draw a fine line between respect and pleasing.

Many people feel it isn't right to take up more than the usual personal space. Take note, it's a relative term and not an absolute, moral issue. So take up as much space as you want. Just don't overdo it and crossover from being a confident sexy alpha stud to an obnoxious son of a whore. There's a big difference.

#2 principle: show your crotch.

Dominant men who attract, seduce and fu*k a lot of girls, have no problem showing their sexuality to the world.

So, don't be afraid to draw attention to the crotch region of your body while you're sitting. Open your legs, maybe put a hand in that region to subconsciously draw attention there; showing a nice belt can help you, too.

Aren't your proud of who you are?

Aren't you proud of your body and your incredibly energetic, attractive sex drive?

Always show your pride: be a MAN, be proud of your sexuality.

Now don't get the wrong idea here. There's a difference between teasing and being Hervert The Pervert.

Teasing is confidently sexy. Hervert The Pervert isn't. For one, don't do this and wear really tight fitting pants that bulge your manliness. That's more of a symptom of an exhibitionist sex maniac than a smooth, confidently suave George Clooney.

Another thing you shouldn't do to look more like Hervert than George is don't obviously point to your cock and worse, look at her with a devilish smile and grin. Again, you'll look more like a stalker than anything.

And of course you don't need to have the length and girth of Jack Napier or Mandingo to confidently expose your crotch region. Remember, self-confidence! A big cock won't do much with miniscule confidence.

Just ask Napoleon Bonaparte.

#3 principle: slow down your movements.

Move slower!

Low status people move quickly and fidgety, they're not comfortable, they don't believe in themselves.

From now on, you'll cut your movements in half.

When you're walking, when you're turning your head, whenever you're moving your body around, do it slower, in half the time you do it right now.

Why do you need to take it slow? A big part of being confident is knowing that you're doing things at your own terms: your time, your way, and your call.

So how do you normally do things when you know you're not pressured by deadlines or you have all the time in the world? That's right – you're not in an effin' hurry! You take your sweet time. You're relaxed.

When you're not in control, guess what – someone or something else is!

When that happens, you don't call the shots and often times, you're hurrying things up because you're dancing to other people's music. You almost always don't have as much time as you'd like to finish your assignment or responsibility. And when you don't have much control over your life, your confidence plummets. And moving very quickly all the time sends the vibe that you're not in control. And that's not confident or sexy.

Another reason why confident alpha males move slower than the omega men is because they're very competent, in bed or otherwise. By taking their time, they show women that they have the ability to get things done well and on time – again, a control issue.

The first reason for moving slow is all about showing authority over one's self and the other is about authority over others, be it people or circumstances, as manifested by results.

So take it slower, badass!

#4 principle: be non-reactive.

Don't react to something outside of your reality. When you're talking with a girl and you hear a siren or a noise, do not turn your head. Stay focused on her and she will feel your masculine, dominant power. She won't look at the source of the noise and she will stay in the moment, following your high status behavior.

Also, be aware of your fidgety movements and correct them: maybe you're touching your hands, or you're moving your feet as a sign of anxiety.

Stop doing that. Be still and relaxed.

With all due respect to women, being a very reactive person is so girly. Nothing else screams "girly man" than being reactive. So why does being reactive scream to a hot woman that you're more feminine than her?

I'd like you to think of a time when most things, if not everything in your life was going as planned. How'd you feel? You probably felt great, steady, calm or at peace. In short, you feel really confident. When one or two curve balls come your way, you're too peaceful to react inappropriately. You react in a calm and collected manner because you know that in the grander scheme of things, you're in control of your life and one or two mishaps won't change that fact.

Now think of a time when most things, if not everything in your life wasn't going your way. How did you feel? Among many other things, I bet you felt you have no control over your life and your situation, which made you high-strung too.

Being reactive to things and people sends the subtle signal to woman that you're highly-strung. Being highly-strung means you feel you generally have little or no control over your life, much less the situation you're in. And that feeling will be strongly transmitted to each and every woman you are planning to score with, which will of course turn them off leaving you as celibate as the Pope.

Try not to be reactive. If you're not yet that confident, don't worry. You can control your impulses and if you do that long and often enough, you'll be able to reprogram your subconscious mind that you really are confident and non-reactive, which will enable you to unconsciously and naturally act that way all the time.

#5 principle: lean back.

Learn to lean back most of the time.

Remember that leaning in is a really low status behavior. Learn to make people, especially girls, feel a subconscious urge to lean towards you, simply by leaning back.

This little trick will change the whole dynamic of your conversations, giving you the power of a badass.

This also means that when you're walking or just standing, you will have your shoulders up and back and your chin up. Just a masculine, healthy posture.

If you're talking to a girl in a loud club (or whatever loud place) then move slowly, lean in, whisper your words into her ear and then go back to leaning back. This will make her come to you whispering in your ear: that's how high status men communicate in loud places, without leaning in in a low status way.

If you want to know the other principles and the great exercises in order to train your Body Language, then check out my book Body Language Training.

What if I told you that with some tips, your standing position could become a real sign of POWER?

What if after reading this short guide, you will be able to attract the girl you want, just sitting in a DOMINANT position or walking like a real badass?

Trust me, body language is really that powerful.

You should already know that human beings are constantly reading situations and other people so that, really quickly, they can know what category put them in: low status, middle status, and high status.

It's just a survival mechanism, because you have to know who has the power and who hasn't. That's something that's been hardwired into us over thousands and thousands of years.

So, most people don't trust words, because we've been taught from a young age to lie with them.

They prefer to read those status cues through the body language: THAT is the honest signal!

High status body language = high status person.

It's that simple, and we trust it.

Once we make the decision or opinion about that person, it's almost impossible for us to break it.

Therefore, your body language is the UNSPOKEN TRUTH.

When you have a high status body language, people conclude that you are in CONTROL of your own reality.

Remember this, my badass friend:

"The body follows the mind, but the mind follows the body even more."

Keeping a high status body language will make you have a high status mindset all the time: this can CHANGE YOUR LIFE for the rest of your days.

Now, this is what you'll discover in Body Language Training:

Why a High Status Body Language Is So Important For Your Life...

The 10 Foundational Principles of High Status Body Language...

My Best Tips and Tricks for Always Displaying a Powerful Body Language...

The Secret Badass Body Language Training...

What Your Walk REVEALS About You...

How To Make Sure She Finds Your Walk Sexually Attractive...

How To Get An Incredible Confidence In Your Walk...

...and much more!

Robert Moore

Check out my other Training Books!

Voice Training: How To Unleash Your Inner Badass Vocal Power With Vocal Exercises, Become A Leader And Get A Deeper Voice In 7 Days Or Less

Voice is one of the most important qualities of a leader.

When you have a POWERFUL voice, life becomes so much easier. Your social life will be much better and your business life will reward you so many times, while girls will be much more attracted to you...

Just imagine yourself at a business meeting: you will be the most valuable guy there, because your voice will be so STRONG and COMMANDING.

Everyone will be raptured by your words.

Political leaders and actors were not born with a powerful voice, they TRAINED it up to that point.

In fact, you don't have a quiet voice, you simply trained it that way.

Now it's time to train it the other way around!

Here Is A Preview Of What You'll Learn In Voice Training...

Why A High-Status Voice Is So Powerful: how to make people know, like and trust you immediately...

The 5 Secret Traits Of A Powerful Voice: capture attention and hold it in a trance-like state every time you open your mouth!

Voice Training: mouth and voice strengthening exercises and tonality secrets used by Hollywood actors to command your audience's attention...

The Power Of Enunciation And Suspense: how to become a master storyteller who holds people rapt, fully engaged and hanging on your every word...

... and much more!

Confidence Training: - Become An Alpha Male by Mastering Your Confidence, Self Esteem & Charisma

Confidence is one of the most important traits to master if you want to succeed in your life.

While you decided to bet on yourself, most men out there are going to continue on their boring lives, controlled by their emotions, like weak little leaves in the wind. You will not.

You're meant for greatness, and I hope this guide will help you reach your goals and transform your life.

In fact, for some guys, mastering their emotions and becoming truly confident will be their graduation from little children to ALPHA MALES. Because from now on, your emotions will work for you, instead of the other way around.

I'm talking about pure, unshakable confidence, which means untouchable indifference and emotional mastery at its finest.

So you can finally start ENJOYING and LIVING LIFE like the king you know you are, staying cool, calm, and collected, no matter what life throws at you.

I'm talking about you finally being able to ask that girl out that you've so desperately wanted to.

I'm talking about you walking straight up to your boss' office and demanding that raise that you deserve (the right way) and getting it within the snap of a finger.

I'm talking about you finally being able to take on ANYTHING that life throws at you, without even flinching.

I'm talking about complete and utter state control over your emotions, for good.

I'm talking about laser-like focus, allowing you to get done in a day what most people get done in a month.

Let's get you going – you're ready for this!